Instinctology®

Pastor Gino,

Thank you for your
Biblically sound guidance
and leadership.

In Christ,

Robin

NOV 2017

Instinctology®

A LEADERSHIP METHOD TO TURN GUT INSTINCTS INTO CONCRETE ACTION

Roben Graziadei, MA

Foreword by
Hyrum Smith, best-selling author of *The Three Gaps*
Co-founder/former CEO FranklinCovey

ISBN: 0692828109
ISBN 13: 9780692828106
Library of Congress Control Number: 2016921581
Roben Graziadei, MA, Littleton, CO

ENDORSEMENTS

"How strong is your intuition? Likely, stronger than you realize. This quick read will help you not only recognize these signs, but learn how to listen more closely to the ones that are subtler. We all have these feelings yet often miss or ignore them, and to our detriment. IN = intuition, inkling, inspiration, inner voice, *Instinctology*®!"
Mary-Jo Kovach
Vice President
Pearson, Inc.

—ᨏ—

"After over forty years of pastoral and family counseling. I have learned to trust my GUT, but never had the right words or concepts to understand more deeply what was happening inside me. I am thankful for *Instinctology*®. As a counselor, coach, and psychologist, Roben's book has given me the insights I need to make wise and right decisions from the inside out. This is a must read for anyone facing tough decisions, internal conflict, or wanting to heal relationships from the inside out. *Instinctology*® is more than a book; it's the beginning of a movement toward soul health!"
Dr. Larry Keefauver
Best-selling Author and International Teacher

—ᨏ—

"A quick read, minded with insight, personal reflections, and opportunities to think about getting more out of your life through learning to trust yourself, stemming from the biblical imperative of 'know thyself.' You can be happier, feel more confidence, and experience greater success taking to heart *Instinctology*®!"

Barry Z. Posner, PhD
Coauthor, *The Leadership Challenge*
Accolti Endowed Professor of Leadership
Dean (1997–2009), Leavey School of Business, Santa Clara University

—⁂—

"I loved the message—trust your gut. Roben tells compelling stories that illustrate the premise of her book *Instinctology*®: *A Leadership Method to Turn GUT Instincts into Concrete Action*. In my experience as a leadership development practitioner, I agree that it all starts with the gut—good, gutsy leaders are clear on their personal values and trust their instincts. She closes each chapter with terrific quotes… some from my favorite writers, like Victor Frankel, Jim Kouzes, and Barry Posner, and others that are a bit of a surprise, like *Alice in Wonderland* and Larry Keefauver. I gained some valuable insights and 'ahas' with this book and will give a second thought to the next time I start to brush someone or something away that I feel—in my gut—I really shouldn't."

Jeni Nichols
Former president and founder
Sonoma Leadership Systems
LEAD2016 Top Partner

—⁂—

"Instinctology® is a twenty-first century must-read! As politics, economics, and war erupt around us, we are inundated with chaos and confusion. *Instinctology®* is a lifestyle that can change lives in a world of turmoil.
John Mucci
Treasurer
Defense Forum Foundation

—֍—

"Through inspiring stories, examples, and practical suggestions, *Instinctology®* deftly illustrates how to achieve success in all areas of your life by following your instincts. The thought-provoking questions and exercises Roben includes in her book are useful tools for anyone wanting to change their lives by practicing and mastering how to tune into, trust, and act upon their instincts. I will recommend this intriguing book to my clients."
Karen Cottengim
Founder and career guide
True North Career Strategy

—֍—

"Instinctology® is a business development game changer. By listening to, trusting, and acting on her GUT instincts, Roben demonstrates a long track record of top performance. Her real life stories and sustained strong performance are evidence of Instinctology® in action!"
Shawn Moon
Coauthor, *Talent Unleashed*
Executive Vice President Leadership and Strategic Accounts
FranklinCovey

—֍—

"Roben gives ROI new meaning, by defining it as ***Return on Instincts***. Roben is evidence of how her definition of ROI, can positively impact your bottom line."
Joshua Covey
Director of Strategy Education Division
FranklinCovey

Dedicated to our beloved Jana Kay,
You are forever in our hearts.

ACKNOWLEDGEMENTS

There are many people I am grateful to for making a difference in my life, which has culminated in the writing of this book. In keeping with the principle of putting first things first, let me begin with three mentors who are remarkable men that live the principles they espouse. The common thread of life-giving leadership is woven throughout the fabric of their lives. In a world of lost leadership, it is comforting to know leaders like you who walk your talk.

Dr. Larry Keefauver, thank you for your guidance. Your charity and bountiful spirit have inspired my writing and moved me. Your contributions to me and so many are far above and beyond anything I could have imagined. You are a life-giving leader, from the GUT! It is an honor and privilege to know you.

Hyrum Smith, when I think of the goodness that you have poured into my life and the lives of so many, my glass is more than half-full. It runneth over with respect and gratitude for the leader that you are. Years ago, when I went to work for you, you mentioned, "God always brings this company the right people." It is humbling to think that I was one of those people who had the honor of learning from you and teaching others. Thank you for allowing me to be a part of the difference you make!

Barry Posner, often I reflect on those days in Palo Alto at TPGLS when we met. Leading adventure courses and teaching the principles from *The Leadership Challenge* were the beginning of a life-altering journey for me. To this day, when I am in a leadership quandary, I pull out my leadership bible, *TLC*, for guidance and accountability. When we worked together on a project for youth leadership, I was reminded that who you are and what you do is truly *The Leadership Challenge* in action. You lead by example, lighting the way for all.

Next, I would like to mention a few colleagues who, in a life-giving way, have exemplified the leadership principles taught by these men. While you may not have thought of it as *Instinctology®*, you have inspired me by living what this book is about.

MJ, I deeply admire your life-giving leadership and professionalism. Your leadership style engenders no fear. We follow you out of love and respect. Debbie, your commitment to making a difference in higher education is unparalleled. Jeni, your dedication to empowering leaders of integrity is life giving! Bill, thank you for taking a chance on me as an author years ago. Craig, thank you for helping me find the light and let it shine! Paula, as my editor, thank you for your devotion to the completion of this book with excellence and love.

Finally, to my devoted friends and family, thank you for helping me traverse what M. Scott Peck calls "the road less traveled."

Mom, you carried yourself with joy in the midst of heartbreak. Miles, you are the love of my life! Scott, you do the right thing when no one is looking. Mary, thank you for tirelessly caring for me when I was ill with life-threatening pneumonia. Carol, you are my everything! Marilyn H., you led my despairing father to healing and redemption. Karen, you are the best career coach! Marilyn B., you held me accountable for writing about *Instinctology®*. Kim and Jan, you make me laugh and never judge me. We always have fun. Neala, thank you for picking up where Mom left off. Mike, your light saved me after Miles passed. Let your light shine! Harry and Jana, you led me to spiritual maturity. Dawson, Dominic, Dillon, Charlie, Colin, and Myla, keep believing in a "happy life." Jennifer, Lisa, and Anne, you are my oxygen! Mark, your integrity runs deep. I am grateful that you are my birth brother and my brother in Christ.

**With much love,
Roben**

The intuitive mind is a sacred gift and the
rational mind is a faithful servant.
We have created a society that honors the
servant and has forgotten the gift.
—BOB SAMPLES

Your time is limited, so don't waste
it living someone else's life.
Don't be trapped by dogma – which is living
with the results of other people's thinking.
Don't let the noise of other's opinions
drown out your own inner voice.
Most important, have the courage to
follow your heart and intuition.
They somehow already know what you truly
want to become. Everything else is secondary.
—STEVE JOBS

Your GUT instincts speak to you.
Listen to them and you will learn to trust them;
Trust them and you will begin to act on them.
Act on them and you will thrive,
Thrive by building a life-giving
and productive lifestyle.
—ROBEN GRAZIADEI

TABLE OF CONTENTS

FOREWORD BY HYRUM SMITH

Winston Churchill has always been one of my heroes. A defining moment in my life was when, as a young man, I heard him speak in London. I have shared this moment of mine many times before, and I would like to share it again because it is relevant to this book. As I listened to Churchill speak toward the end of his life, he indicated that he had been obsessed with the need to make a difference on the planet.

If anyone has made a difference in this world, Winston Churchill has. He probably saved the free world during World War II. As I listened to him speak that day, his words entered my heart and lit a flame. It was as if a baton had been passed to me that day, and I decided, "You know what? I'm going to make a difference too."

I have strived to do that from that point on. One of the vehicles along my journey that allowed me to make a positive difference in people's lives was the creation of the Franklin Quest Co., which later became FranklinCovey. This is where I met Roben Graziadei. Our business was growing very fast, and we needed to find dynamic, articulate, and passionate presenters in order to meet the high demand for our seminars and time- and life-management tools. Roben was a Godsend. She became a senior consultant and was one of the best presenters at Franklin. She was confident and passionate about our principles and our product. She helped move forward my quest to make a difference in the world.

Now she is making a difference in her own right. She is the founder and president of Net Result$, LLC. She trains and consults for individuals and companies all over the world to develop strong leadership skills, increasing their productivity and their bottom line.

Which brings us to her book *Instinctology®: A Leadership Method to Turn GUT Instincts into Concrete Action*. I had not seen Roben in many years when, via modern-day networking technology, we were able to reconnect several months ago. She said she was writing a book and told me a little about it. I was intrigued. She allowed me to read a rough draft, and today I am honored to write the foreword. The trademarked term Instinctology® is in part defined by Roben as **the study and habit of listening to, trusting, and acting on your GUT instincts.**

There is more, but I don't want to spoil the discovery. I especially appreciate that GUT is an acronym. Read on to learn what that acronym represents. I particularly wanted to focus on the word *habit* in her definition. There is a poem called "Habit" by an unknown author that has impacted me over my life. It goes like this:

Habit

I am your constant companion; I am your greatest
helper or your heaviest burden.
I will push you onward or drag you down to failure.

I am completely at your command.
Half the things you do
You might just as well turn over to me,
And I will do them quickly and correctly.

I am easily managed; you must merely be firm with me,
Show me exactly how you want something done,
And I will do it automatically

I am not a machine,
Though I work with all the precision of a machine
Plus the intelligence of a man.

You may run me for profit or run me for ruin;
It makes no difference to me.
I am the servant of all great men;
Alas, of all failures as well.

Take me, train me, be firm with me,
And I will place the world at your feet.
Be easy with me, and I will destroy you.

Who am I?

I am habit.
—Unknown

We make habits every day, sometimes without even realizing it. Our habits can make us or break us. If you incorporate the Instinctology® lifestyle habit as explained in this book, it will make you. It's as simple as that. I have taught all of my adult life that there are natural laws or true principles that govern behavior and its outcomes that are just as real as the natural law of gravity; when applied, they will bring inner peace and a balanced life, which in turn leads to more productivity and success. Roben Graziadei's *Instinctology®: A Leadership Method to Turn GUT Instincts into Concrete Action* is filled with many of those true principles.

As I understand Instinctology®, it is not only a way of living, but also a mentality that allows you to tap into and use your GUT as a tool to bridge what I call the gaps in our lives. You can become your best self as well as achieve your vision or reach your goals, and lead others to do the same. By living the Instinctology® lifestyle, you can make a difference in the world around you.

Best wishes to everyone who reads this book. You are about to begin an impactful journey that will enrich the rest of your life.

Hyrum W. Smith
Co-founder/former CEO FranklinCovey
Best-selling author of *The 10 Natural Laws of Time and Life Management, The Three Gaps,* and *You Are What You Believe*

My forty-year career is coming down
to a three-second decision.
—**Sully, US Airways captain of the
"Miracle on the Hudson"**

Alex Parish, your gut instincts make
you an excellent FBI agent!
—*Quantico*, **an ABC television series**

I had a dream in which I was given the lottery
numbers. So I bought a ticket with those numbers.
—**2016 $5 million lottery winner**

I told my manager, "My instincts are telling
me to call this CAO right now."
I pulled the car over and made the phone
call. The CAO answered. We are now
working with this CAO's institution.
—**Roben Graziadei**

While in the midst of battle in the Vietnam War,
my sergeant told our platoon to head left. In a split
second, my instincts told me to head right, so I did.
The rest of the platoon went left with the sergeant.
They walked right into a trap and
were blown to pieces.
—**US Army soldier**

My instincts told me to clean house with the
executive team I inherited when becoming the
new CEO of a high-tech firm. I ignored my
instincts and have paid for it dearly ever since.
—**CEO of a Fortune 500 Silicon
Valley high-tech company**

Have you ever longed to…

- Inspire a shared vision resulting in laser-focused results?
- Be more decisive with follow-through and time-sensitive action(s)?
- Improve the quality of your relationships, both personal and professional?
- Find closure and freedom from past wounds and traumas?
- Enhance your work life and/or find a better career/employment fit?
- Increase your finances in an economic world of uncertainty?
- Maintain peace and calm as chaos swirls all around you?
- Increase your confidence?
- Regain control of your life?
- Manage your losses and disappointments better?
- Increase your productivity?
- Bridge your three gaps—values, beliefs, and time—both individually and corporately?
- Seize those life-giving moments that you have been missing?
- Turn your GUT instincts into concrete action?

Complete this sentence:

If only I had trusted my GUT instincts when_____
_____.

And the day came when the risk
to remain tight in a bud was more
painful than the risk it took to blossom.
—**ANAIS NIN**

The sun can't force itself onto the shade:
When the shade is ready, it will receive the sun.
—**ROBEN GRAZIADEI**

PREFACE

D o you want to make a difference? Are you looking for a game-changer? If so, Instinctology® is for you. I invite you to lead from your GUT instincts and will teach you how to do so.

As the final edits were being completed for this book, something happened to me that I want you to know about. What I am about to share with you is evidence of Instinctology® in action and at its best.

Having contracted pneumonia in both of my lungs, my friend Mary rushed me to the emergency room. I was immediately hospitalized for twelve days, and I spent ten of those days in the ICU. After being released from the hospital, my doctor told me the pneumonia that I had was life-threatening and had been fatal for many patients. While in the ICU, the doctors and nurses were skeptical about my recovery. In the end, the doctors applauded me for "dodging a bullet." One doctor exclaimed, "It is not your time to die. Someone wants you alive!"

This life-threatening experience put everything that I teach about Instinctology® to the test for me. I am deeply grateful for the stories and lessons I learned that you will read about in this book, which, it turns out, prepared me for this ICU event. While in the ICU, I felt a peace that passes all understanding, along with confidence and hope as I applied my life-giving GUT instincts moment by moment. With eight doctors standing over me, calling in the chaplain and asking me for my power of attorney, I was able to rise above the emotions of this immediate threat. After they left the room, I cried out to God for his/her perfect will to come forth for me, be it life or be it death.

The next morning, my health had improved significantly. The doctors moved me from the ICU to a regular room. Ten months later, my lung capacity scores had improved by 55 percent. Prior to maturing and living an Instinctology® lifestyle, I would have been an emotional mess and likely taken it out on the good people around me. Not this time. Immediately, I turned my GUT instincts into concrete action, as taught in this book. In so doing, I traversed this life-threatening experience with a calm confidence and galvanizing hope.

I have coined and trademarked the word Instinctology®.

Instinctology® is the study and habit of listening to, trusting, and acting on your GUT instincts.

My book is titled *Instinctology®: A Leadership Method to Turn GUT Instincts into Concrete Action.* We all have these instincts; we were born with them. Yet, Western culture has taught us to suppress them or ignore them altogether. In this book, you will learn about your GUT instincts and how to listen to, trust, and act on them even in the face of the daily internal and external distractions that at times bombard all of us.

We live in a data-driven world. I am *not* proposing that you negate or ignore numerical/statistical data. I am simply recommending that you include this powerful, game-changing data point, your GUT instinct, as a variable in your decision making process. We have become so dependent on statistical data and information that organizations, families, governments, and relationships are bleeding from a lack of human touch. Let that human element include your life-giving GUT instincts as a data point in your business model, leadership practices, and relational quest. Simply put, numerical/statistical data can be manipulated to validate any point the peanut counters want to make. Not so with your life-giving GUT instincts. When you practice Instinctology® as a part of your leadership style, you are entering the no-spin zone!

We are inundated with constant external distractions from the Internet, mass media, and religious, educational, governmental, and corporate messaging. Many of us struggle with negative internal scripts. Perhaps, like me, you may have adhered to these messages at the expense of listening to and giving honor to your GUT instincts, leading from the inside out.

My colleague asked me if this was the same as blind faith. No, not really; it is trusting your GUT instincts with your eyes wide open and turning them into action! We all have them. We simply need to train ourselves to acknowledge, trust, and act on them.

When I was writing this book, person after person would say to me, "If only I would have trusted to my gut when…" C-suite, small business, community, and family leaders would tell me their worst decisions and biggest mistakes came when they ignored, discounted, or rejected their GUT instincts. Some of their best outcomes came when they took a stand for their GUT instincts, fighting for the highest good for themselves, others, and their organizations in the face of adversity or otherwise.

How many times have you regretted not listening to or trusting your GUT? This book will inspire you with Instinctology® stories and the acronym ACT—three simple steps to practice Instinctology®. I like to think of leaders who practice Instinctology® as gutsy leaders! It takes guts to listen to, trust, and act on your GUT instincts. For me, the rewards for doing so have far outweighed the risks of not doing so. The return on my instincts has improved the return on my investments, financial and otherwise. Including my GUT instincts as a data point has truly been a life-altering and empowering game-changer and has given a new meaning to ROI! I am convinced that you too will embrace this new term for ROI (Return on Instincts) as you read the real life and miraculous stories that I share with you in this book.

Go with me directly to the radical, root denotation of the word *instinct* as defined by the dictionary:

> **in·stinct** n [ME, fr. L instinctus impulse, fr. instinguere to incite; akin
> to L instigare to instigate] (15c)
> 1: a natural or inherent aptitude, impulse, or capacity <had an instinct for the right word> 2 a: a largely inheritable and unalterable tendency of an organism to make a complex and specific response to environmental stimuli without involving reason 2 b: behavior that is mediated by reactions below the conscious level[1]

Now, bear with me just a moment as I briefly bring to light a few of my basic assumptions so that you clearly understand where I am going with my definition of Instinctology®. As denoted in the above dictionary definition, an instinct is inherent aptitude, which is largely inheritable and unalterable, being a behavior controlled and influenced by reactions below the conscious level, i.e. the subconscious and unconscious.

In this book, my focus will be on how your subconscious emotions, scripts, attitudes, habits, motives, intentions, beliefs, and thoughts rise to your consciousness. Initially they were imbedded in your subconscious—created and imparted to you by the Creator, implanted in your subconscious by parental figures as you matured through childhood, and formulated by your experiences and

1 Merriam-Webster (2009-06-12). *Merriam-Webster's Collegiate Dictionary*, 11th Edition (Kindle Locations 608328-608344). Merriam-Webster, Inc. Kindle Edition.

defining moments. These instincts can be known and understood. Instinctology® can become the tool for bridging the gap between your subconscious and conscious mind.

In his book *The 3 Gaps*, Hyrum Smith addresses how the values, beliefs, and time gaps within individuals and organizations might thwart one's success and productivity. In Section II of this book, I will teach you how to use Instinctology® as one essential tool to help bridge these gaps.

Think of it this way. Your subconscious instincts constitute the soil in which all your conscious behaviors—verbal and nonverbal—arise and manifest, thereby impacting and influencing others and you. In the popular documentary *What the Bleep Do We Know*, Dr. Joe Dispenza states that a healthy human brain can process 400 billion bits of information per second. However, we are only conscious of about 2,000 of those 400 billion bits of information. In simpler terms, he is telling you that most of the information of reality is processed by your unconscious mind.[2]

Now, I am not attempting to get all that psychological, scientific, or mental on you, but I do want you to come to understand how your mind housed within your "computer-brain" is working, and beyond that, how the operating system, programs, and software in your mind's subconscious are displaying what you and others see and hear on the screen of your conscious.

A brief picture painted for you here may help. While I write this book, I am using a computer, which is running millions of operations outside of my immediate view of what I am seeing on my computer screen as I type. Decades of research, programming work, hardware engineering, and manufacturing have made possible the wonderful mechanism I am using to write and thereby

---

2 http://www.getniusawakening.com/genius-brain/subconscious-mind-controls-behavior

communicate my thoughts and concepts about Instinctology® to you in this book.

I know you get it, as you very likely use the "subconscious" technology behind your computer, tablet, smartphone, television, car, appliances, etc. to serve you as you consciously live out your life.

Here's the bottom line. As gutsy leaders, we would like first to understand and then to use our inherent, imparted, and inbred instincts to serve us constructively, positively, creatively, and dynamically so that we can live life fully, prosperously, successfully, productively, and joyfully. This book will equip and empower you to do just that!

Defining Instinctology®

Here is my *Merriam-Webster*-style definition of Instinctology®:

The study and habit of listening to, trusting, and acting on your GUT instincts.

Furthermore, I define our GUT instincts as:

- **G**od's—your higher power
- **U**tmost—the highest good for yourself and others
- **T**ruth—within you, leading from the inside out

As I reflect on how I have grown and matured, Instinctology® has propelled me forward and ultimately helped me to rise out of the ashes and make a positive difference. I have gone from depressed and hopeless to being at peace and full of life and hope…from suffering with poor self-esteem to a gracious confidence, from struggling financially to financial abundance, from being complacent about my work and career to being a top producer, from being vulnerable to manipulation to standing my ground, from victimized to victorious, and finally from ashes to beauty.

After I define what GUT instincts are, I will then share personal, real-life stories of amazing, even miraculous outcomes that have resulted throughout my life by simply tuning into, trusting, and acting on my GUT instincts. Like me, I am sure that you have also desired to and struggled to heal from losses or past trauma and increase the quality of your life. *Instinctology®: A Leadership Method to Turn GUT Instincts into Concrete Action* can help you achieve your dreams and goals beyond your highest and greatest imaginings.

Here are those questions again. Have you ever longed to…

- Inspire a shared vision resulting in laser-focused results?
- Be more decisive with follow-through and time-sensitive action(s)?
- Improve the quality of your relationships, both personal and professional?
- Find closure and freedom from past wounds and traumas?
- Enhance your work life and/or find a better career/employment fit?
- Increase your finances in an economic world of uncertainty?
- Maintain peace and calm as chaos swirls all around you?
- Increase your confidence?
- Regain control of your life?
- Manage your losses and disappointments better?
- Increase your productivity?
- Bridge your three gaps—values, beliefs, and time—both individually and corporately
- Seize those life-giving moments that you have been missing?
- Turn your GUT instincts into concrete action?

Have you wished for a second chance to complete this sentence differently?

If only I had trusted my GUT instincts when_____
_____.

In my life's journey, I have had to face every one of these questions and more.

It is my profound hope that you will also rise above the murk and mire; the noise pollution; the oppressors, bullies, and controllers; the manipulators; the religious, governmental, and mental scripts; and the conventional wisdom implanted during childhood and through mass media. I envision that you will stop wallowing with the turkeys and begin to soar on wings like an eagle's, fulfilling your inborn and created destiny. By living in the flow of your GUT instincts, you can live more abundantly, lead more effectively, love more deeply, serve more purely, enjoy inner peace, and experience more life-giving energy so that you too **will rise above mere survival mode, thrive, and live life fully, joyfully, and prosperously. You will stand up like never before for the highest good of yourself and others.**

Lead from your GUT instincts.

With much love,
Roben

P.S. You can watch Roben's video where she shares this preface at **www.instinctology.com**.

SECTION I

Life begins at the end of your comfort zone.
—Neale Donald Walsch

Peace, it does not mean to be in a place where
there is no noise, trouble, or hard work.
It means to be in the midst of those things
and still be calm in your heart.
—Unknown

Stand Up. Gutsy Leaders Serve...

One evening, after his young students at the underground semi-nary of Finkenwalde had finished their supper, Dietrich Bonhoeffer went alone to the kitchen to wash the dishes.

He began the work alone; then he requested the help of his pupils. But the seminarians did not budge, leaving Bonhoeffer alone scrubbing silverware. When no one offered to serve alongside him, he locked the door. When the students realized what he had done, they felt badly and finally offered to help. The door, however, remained locked, and Bonhoeffer finished the work alone.

His lesson was simple: service and leadership go together, and true service does not stem from lazy pity.[3]

3 Chris Nye in *Leadership Journal*, http://www.christianitytoday.com/le/2015/april-onlineonly/leading-likebonhoeffer.html

INTRODUCTION

Instinctology®—Gutsy Leaders Turn their GUT Instincts into Concrete Action

Now that I have told you where I am coming from, let me tell you where I am taking you on this journey of unpacking, uncovering, and understanding *Instinctology®—A Leadership Method to Turn GUT Instincts into Concrete Action.*

Instinctology®, n.: The study and habit of listening to, trusting, and acting on your GUT instincts.

How will this improve your leadership serve, return, and winning volley? Tom Peters, author of *In Search of Excellence*, also wrote a book titled *Leadership Is Everyone's Business.* Our culture is bleeding from a lack of trusted leadership. One might ask: Where have all the leaders gone? You may even be asking yourself: What might I do to be a more effective leader of myself, my family, my church, my community, the corporation that I work for, and my circle of influence? As I have matured and grown, I have come to one conclusion:

**In order to lead others more effectively,
I must first lead myself more effectively,
From the inside out!**

"To lead or not to lead?" That is the question. This is where Instinctology® comes to the rescue. It takes GUTS to effectively lead in today's complex world. My friend Hyrum Smith, Co-founder/former CEO of FranklinCovey, in his latest book *The 3 Gaps*, has identified three gaps that keep individuals and organizations from inner peace and quantum productivity. For me, Instinctology® is a tool that has helped me bridge these gaps. You are surely familiar with Steven R Covey's work, *The Seven Habits of Highly Effective People*, and Steven M R Covey's work *The Speed of Trust*. One might say that Instinctology® is the foundation of self-trust and an additional habit of a highly effective person. Finally, with regard to recognizing and unleashing great talent, imagine the possibilities when employees learn how to tune into their GUT instincts. What kind of creativity, resourcefulness and ownership might be unleashed? What would your organization look like if your employees were engaged at this level?

When I listen to, trust, and act on my GUT instincts, it fortifies me with clarity and conviction to stand up and lead myself and others more effectively. It is this backbone of listening to my GUT instincts for the highest good of myself and others that has improved my leadership and quality of life. Is Instinctology® the missing piece to twenty-first-century leadership? I have observed that many of our famous and infamous leaders listen to the plethora of outside voices, corporate and shareholder pressures, national and global politics, religious and peer pressures, and even internal negative scripts more than they listen to their convictions and act on their conscience.

Where have all the *effective* leaders gone? The good news is that you and I are here, now. We are standing at home plate in the field of leadership, ready to hit the ball. I love leadership author John Maxwell's fantastic story about his nephew, Eric, playing little league baseball. Here is just a snapshot for you:

Eric was afraid of swinging the bat. He didn't want to strike out. Time and time again, John watched his nephew cower at the plate.

Then Uncle (and self-appointed coach) John started encouraging and urging his nephew to swing the bat. Why? Because when Uncle John started encouraging Eric, he knew that by swinging the bat his nephew increased the odds of the ball hitting the bat. And, if the ball in some wondrous, rare, and exciting moment should hit the bat and be fair, the odds of Eric successfully reaching base were quite good, since many of those very young players lacked the skill to catch and effectively throw the ball to first base and tag Eric out. Furthermore, if Eric safely reached base (and he was a very fast runner), he might just keep running, circling the bases, and make it home, scoring a run!

By reading this book, you are standing at home plate in life's essential game of leadership and swinging the bat. I am coaching, mentoring, encouraging, and cheering for you to practice Instinctology® and gutsy leadership, to develop your leadership skills so that you will stop striking out and start hitting the ball effectively, thereby becoming a successful, prospering, exemplary leader, achieving the outcomes and results that you quest for.

We are swinging the bat. Starting right here, right now, we can unite to make a positive difference. My high school yearbook writings are coming back to me. The yearbook theme that I came up with for our senior annual, was **"We Are One Together,"** meaning that we are distinct individuals, and when united with a shared vision, we are one.

Each of us has the gift of our GUT instincts. I can teach you how to listen to, trust, and act on your GUT instincts. Embracing this as a shared vision together, we can make Instinctology® a societal norm and effective leadership style. As stand-up leaders tuning into our instincts, we can bring ourselves and our families, churches, communities, governments, and corporations back to a place of strength, prosperity, wisdom, and love. A gutsy leader's role and his or her decisions are not driven by or made at the expense of others for gain or greed. Rather, a gutsy leader's roles and decisions are driven by and made based on their GUT instincts, with the highest good for ourselves and others in mind. It's not a contradiction to say that gutsy leaders have the courage to lead through service with a willingness to stand up alone, no matter what the sacrifice, as exemplified by Deitrich Bonhoeffer (note the quote at the beginning of this chapter). Servant-quality leadership has its cost too. Ultimately, for Bonhoeffer, gutsy leadership bought him a ticket to Auschwitz and death in opposition to Hitler and Nazism. Yet what a legacy he left us with!

CHAPTER 1

Stories of Historical Leaders Who Turned Their GUT Instincts into Concrete Action

et's take a moment to reflect on a few gutsy leaders throughout history. Gutsy leaders are stand-up leaders. They are the people in history that made a huge difference by listening to that still, small voice within them, even when—no, especially when—they were bombarded with outside voices and/or inner scripts that could potentially cloud their judgment or thinking. Three of our most beloved historical leaders are remembered for standing up and leading based on their internal voices, convictions, and consciences. They tuned into, trusted, and ultimately acted on their instincts, leaving a legacy for generations to come.

President Franklin D. Roosevelt's Instinctology® Story

Prior to 1955, when television was introduced into our homes, we relied on the telephone party line for mass communication. There was no television, no Internet, no social media. In fact, in 1941, when Pearl Harbor was attacked, due to limited technology and media channels, President Franklin D. Roosevelt had minimal and time-delayed information regarding the attack. In order to prepare his speech to the nation, he needed confirmation that the attack was in fact real and not a rumor. His speechwriter was not available at the time. Therefore, he wrote his speech to the nation with limited data or input from others. At one point, his advisors seized an opportunity to rewrite his speech, with the goal of dictating to the president what his address to the nation should say. Yes, they were "shoulding" on him! His critics used this moment to stealthily discredit Roosevelt and the speech he had penned. However, Roosevelt stuck to his convictions. He personally wordsmithed the speech the advisors had rewritten. The result is that his speech has become one of the top hundred speeches in history, with its memorable opening line:

> "Yesterday, December 7, 1941, a date
> that will live in infamy…"

In so doing, Franklin D. Roosevelt became one of our most beloved presidents. His legacy as a leader moved him to stand up and lead in the face of opposition and pressure, and he will continue to inspire generations to come. I would call President Roosevelt an Instinctology® gutsy leader.

Martin Luther King's Instinctology® Story

Dr. Martin Luther King Jr., also one of America's most beloved leaders, left an unparalleled legacy as a gutsy, stand-up leader. After police attacked a nonviolent protest on March 7, 1965, on March 9 Martin Luther King led demonstrators in another nonviolent protest march in which he stopped the protestors midmarch, knelt down, and prayed. Upon praying and quietly taking in the wisdom of God's Utmost Truth within him, he decided to turn the marchers around and led them back to Selma.

He was criticized and challenged for this decision. Yet, it was this decision that led to President Johnson's televised address in support of King's cause. This led to a federal sanction that allowed the launch of a peaceful, five-day, fifty-four-mile march from Selma to Montgomery on March 21, 1965. I would say that at the time, though he may not have thought of it in these words, Dr. King was an Instinctology® gutsy leader who served others with courage and, as did Bonhoeffer, paid the ultimate price of leadership with his life.

Princess Diana's Instinctology® Story

Let's turn now to one of the world's most beloved leaders of all time: the "people's princess," Princess Diana. In the face of persecution and adversity from the royal monarchy, the people's princess found her own voice. Always gracious, Princess Diana was truly a stand-up leader with GUTs. Drawing on her reservoir of grace and strength and trusting her instincts, she led societal change. Not so much from her role in the royal family—what I think of as her positional power—but rather from her internal strength, her personal power. All of us have GUT instincts, regardless of our position, fame, physical appearances, etc. You might say, "Yes, but she had the backing of the royal family." In fact, she did not have the royal family's backing.

Throughout history, the royal family of Great Britain led from the luxuries of the palace. Princess Diana changed all of that by leading in ways that were radically different from royal tradition, perhaps paving the way for our now cherished and embraced Princess Catherine. One of the leadership moments that she is most famous for is in "1987, when so many still believed that AIDS could be contracted through casual contact, Princess Diana sat on the sickbed of a man with AIDS and held his hand. She showed the world that people with AIDS deserve no isolation, but compassion and kindness. It helped change world opinion and gave hope to people with AIDS, with an outcome of saved lives of people at risk" (blog for LPO 3450, Leadership Theory and Behavior, at Vanderbilt University, taught by Professor Jane Robbins).

Many examples are reported of Princess Diana's leadership moments that we could recount. However, those moments were only afforded to her and the world by her moral convictions, conscience, and willingness to serve common people in an unassuming manner. Dare I say, they were fueled by her listening to, trusting, and acting on her instincts instead of succumbing to global, political, and royal pressures! Princess Diana was a strong example of Instinctology® and gutsy leadership.

These leaders, while in the midst of chaos and with pressures and violence looming around them, paused and listened to, trusted, and acted on their internal convictions and conscience. They did not succumb to the external distractions or pressures. These leaders, along with many other women and men throughout history, were gutsy leaders that stood up and led. That left their imprints and legacies on this planet for all time. Unlike now, in the twenty-first century, these earlier leaders only had to tune out all of the external critics and internal voices at their *immediate disposal*.

Today's leaders, be they found in the family, church, community, government, or corporate world, are challenged by an influx of constant noise pollution from television, radio, newsprint, social media, peer pressure, the Internet—the list goes on. We, along with them, need Instinctology® as an essential tool to add to our toolbox in order to lead ourselves and others more effectively and to turn our GUT instincts into action.

I am your Instinctology® coach and cheerleader, here to advocate that you listen to, trust, and act on your instincts. This book is about how doing so has led to success and prosperity for myself and others. This book also addresses how *not* doing so can result in destruction and harm. Those times that you or I ignore our GUT instincts can result in the most painful moments or seasons of our lives. My heart's desire is to spare you such pain. However, as Kouzes and Posner refer to the concept of "failing forward" in their book *The Leadership Challenge*, we too can learn from our mistakes. By failing forward, we can excel. Instinctology® is the tool I have relied on for both my success and for helping me turn my failures into triumphant victories. I have moved from struggling in mere survival mode to journeying toward thriving materially, physically, psychologically, and spiritually! Read on as I share personal Instinctology® success stories and an Instinctology® failing forward story. In Section II of this book, I will teach you how to turn your GUT instincts into concrete action using the acronym ACT.

A word of caution is in order here. Please note that your GUT instincts as defined in this book will never lead you to intentionally harm yourself or another. Leaders who practice Instinctology® do not lead with the implicit motive of seizing personal profit and gain at the expense of others' loss and demise. Your GUT instincts will have the highest good of yourself and others as the goal. For all the psychopaths, sociopaths, narcissists, or just plain jerks or jerkettes out there, your GUT instincts will never guide you to harm yourself or another person, or to wield your personal or positional power for gain to the detriment or at the expense of others.

That said, I deeply desire to equip, strengthen, empower, and support you in becoming the Instinctology® gutsy leader you were created and destined to be by embracing one of your most empowering gifts, your GUT instincts. Join me in this journey of taking a deeper dive into understanding what GUT instincts are and how to embed them irrevocably into your mind, taking Instinctology® from a subconscious gift to a conscious commitment, to a daily habit, to an empowering and productive lifestyle. Listening to, trusting, and acting on my GUT ultimately has improved the quality of my life and allowed me to move from mere survival mode to thriving—like the phoenix rising out of the ashes, to rise above it all! Now let's turn to stories that illuminate the process of living out of our GUT.

On this voyage, our progress is not
measured by the standards of this world,
but by the quality of our character.
—**Erwin Raphael McManus**

A true leader has the confidence to stand alone,
the courage to make tough decisions,
and the compassion to listen to the needs of others.
[S]he does not set out to be a leader
but becomes one by the quality of his[/her]
actions and the integrity of his[/her] intent.
—**Anonymous**

Love and truth form a good leader;
Sound leadership is founded on loving integrity.
—**Proverbs 20:28**

Fear brings illusions; illusions bring doubts.
Doubts bring confusion, and confusion brings fear.
Thus the cycle of darkness regenerates itself.
Peace brings stillness. Stillness brings knowing.
Knowing brings truth;
Truth brings freedom.
Freedom brings joy.
Joy brings love.
And so it is we grow in light.
Thus the cycle of light regenerates itself.
—**Unknown**

See beyond the ordinary.
—**James Baldwin**

CHAPTER 2

The Author's Instinctology® Stories

This chapter is about how trusting my GUT improved my outcomes with financial wealth/ROI, family/relationships, business and career success, service to others, personal enjoyment, and spiritual/physical health.

Recently, I had my car serviced, which included rotating and putting on new tires. As I drove out of the repair shop, the difference in the drive and ride was undeniable. Our wheel of life includes many spokes that might require some repair and rotating for a smoother ride. In this chapter, I will share an Instinctology® success story for a few spokes on the Wheel of Life: Financial/Wealth, Family/Relationships, Business/Career, Service to Others, Personal Enjoyment, and Spiritual/Physical Health. The wheels of my life have gone from running out of air, or hobbling along with broken spokes, to a smooth ride that comes with the best set of freshly rotated Pirellis on a Mercedes Benz or BMW.

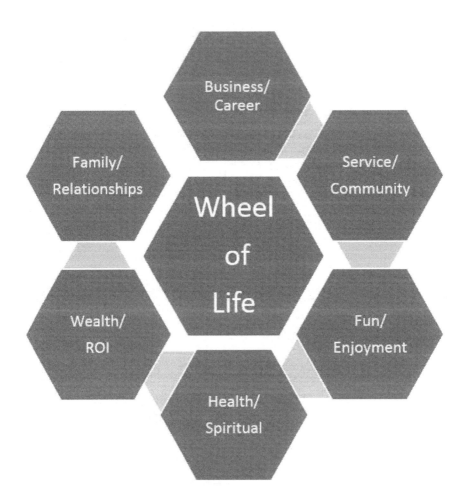

Join me now as I share some of my stories with you. As you read this, ask yourself: What is your Instinctology® story? Take some time to dissect each story. While digesting each one, pay close attention to the specific actions that I took based on Instinctology® prompting me to move from a GUT instinct to a tangible action, resulting in a measurable outcome. We will start with a few stories about financial wealth.

How Turning My GUT Instincts into Concrete Action Has Increased My Financial Wealth/ROI

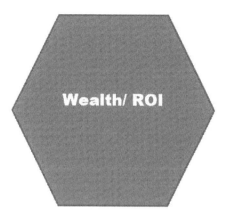

A Real Estate Instinctology® Success Story

Time and again, I have personally experienced financial increase by tuning into, trusting, and acting on my GUT instincts, God's Utmost Truth within me.

Many years back, having purchased a home in northern California and owning it for a little over two years, circumstances arose that led me to sell this home. The market had significantly declined since I purchased the home. This could have resulted in a steep financial loss to me.

Providentially, one night via a dream, my GUT instincts whispered to me the price I needed to list the home for.

Immediately upon awaking from my sleep, I wrote down what I call my "first light thoughts," which included the asking price given to me in my dream. This asking price was significantly higher than the appraisal and market value.

After meeting with a dozen or so Realtors, all of whom turned me down to list at my desired asking price, one insightful Realtor accepted and listed the home at the asking price that I wanted, based on my dream. I had explained to each Realtor that the asking price came to me in a dream and that I believe we all have GUT instincts we ignore. My life mission is to help myself and others excel by honoring our GUT instincts. They must have thought I was a lunatic! That is, until three weeks later, when a buyer called and made a cash offer to purchase the property at my full asking price. She even signed an appraisal waiver, allowing me and my Realtor to legally sell the house at an above-market price point. Talk about giving new meaning to ROI (Return on Instincts)!

Now, you may think, "Right, Roben, San Francisco real estate is always a moneymaker. Or you got lucky on this one." Let me remind you:

1) The market was significantly down from two years before, when I bought the home.
2) If I did get lucky, it was only because I listened to and took a stand for the asking price given to me by my GUT instincts in a dream.

I had to be willing to be a gutsy leader, to stand up for myself, and to take a stand for my GUT by sticking firm to my dream and financial plan. When Realtors mocked me or scoffed at me, it rolled off my back like water off a duck. I had 100 percent confidence that my GUT instincts were correct. I was not about to let the doubts or negative attitudes of others keep me from the financial increase that my GUT instincts had informed me of in a dream.

Over time, this type of financial increase has become a pattern for me. By committing to and practicing Instinctology® as a lifestyle, the numerous stories that I have to share similar to this one would be a book in and of themselves. Before moving on, please allow me to share a few more success stories regarding financial increase.

More Real Estate Instinctology® Success Stories

Recently, I was given a career opportunity that would require me to relocate to the state of Colorado. I had absolutely no emotional peace about relocating, yet my GUT instincts kept leading me in that direction. I spoke with my pastor at the time, who was as puzzled about my quandary as I was—for the notion of inner peace is often espoused as a basic principle for sound decision making. My internal struggle ensued, as historically inner peace was a deciding factor in making a wise decision. This time was different. I had no peace about moving to Colorado. Yet, each time I had a GUT instinct that I tuned into, trusted, and acted on, it manifested into real-life miracles. That confirmed that the move to Colorado may have its challenges, yet surely it was meant to be and ultimately was God's Utmost Truth (my GUT instinct) for me in this particular situation.

One of the challenges was to sell my condominium in Kansas City, Missouri, so that I could roll the money over into a home in Colorado. Well, let me tell you, the Kansas City real estate market at is best is nothing like the San Francisco real estate market at its worst!

To break even on the sale of my Kansas City home, I would need to sell it without a Realtor's fee. Using my rational head and business mind-set, I started googling data on residential sales, price points, trends, etc. Being the businesswoman that I am, I began making a spreadsheet and checking it twice. In the midst of doing so, I stood up from my desk and walked to the kitchen to pour myself another cup of coffee. As I walked back toward my desk, my GUT instincts whispered to me, "Go to the

Peanut," which was the neighborhood bar a block from my home. I thought, "What, go to the Peanut?"

Then I remembered how many times I had been blessed with financial increase by tuning into, trusting, and acting on this inner voice that I call my GUT instinct. Immediately I obeyed my inner voice, my higher self, talking to me. I put the pen down. I closed Google and my spreadsheet built on sound data and research, which told me there was no way I could break even on this house unless I sold it without needing to pay a Realtor's fee. I walked out of my home to the Peanut neighborhood bar. The Peanut is to Kansas City what Cheers is to Boston. When I walked in, the bartender would shout my name and direct me to an open barstool. I had no idea why I was there, except that my GUT instincts tapped me on the shoulder and urged me to go.

Upon sitting on my frequently appointed barstool and placing my beer-and-burger order, the man sitting next to me shouted out to the bartender this request: "Say, Brian, we are visiting from San Francisco, and our daughter will be going to school here at UMKC. Rents around here are really high. We were hoping to buy her a condo within walking distance to campus. Do you know of anyone around here selling a condo?"

I smiled to myself, thanked God for my GUT instincts, turned to the man, and said, "Well, as a matter of fact, I am selling my condo, but have not listed it yet. Perhaps we could work out a deal whereby we forego a Realtor's fee, which will give you a better price on the condo." Long story short, he, his wife, and his daughter saw and bought the condo within three weeks of our meeting at the Peanut. I sold my condo without a Realtor, based on the data from my research indicating it would be the only way to break even. More importantly, it was based on the data from my GUT instincts, which whispered to me to stop by the neighborhood bar that night.

No joke! That is exactly what happened. Thus my encouragement to you to add Instinctology® to your toolbox. Utilize data given not only by research, facts, logic, and reason, but also by your GUT instincts. In this case, the below equation was the outcome:

Leading by my GUT instincts + facts based on
research = financial increase/ROI (Return on Instincts)

As it turned out, I not only broke even on the sale of my condo in a down Kansas City market, but also the home I bought in Colorado has over time increased in market value by 40 percent. This financial gain was a direct result of listening to, trusting, and acting on my GUT instincts. I had not shared this with you yet, but it was my GUT instincts that led me to the neighborhood and home that I bought when relocating to Colorado.

A Family/Relationships Instinctology® Success Story—How Listening to, Trusting, and Acting on My GUT Instincts Led to Healing a Relationship

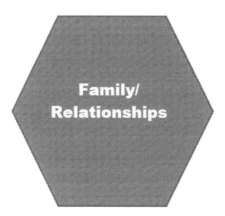

One of the greatest outcomes from trusting my GUT instincts is a blessing that I will forever and always be grateful for. Having once married my college sweetheart, we had been divorced for over twenty years. I am the type of woman that does not interfere with her ex-husband's current marriage, so I withheld my urges to reach out to him over the years for healing and closure. To me, marriage is a sacred institution. While our marriage failed, I did not want to do anything that might hurt his second marriage by reaching out to him.

I went on with my life, which, twenty years later, led to our re-uniting based on me (and he as well) tuning into, trusting, and acting on our GUT instincts.

It was the height of summer, and I was living in Colorado. My business took me to Kansas City every few months. The company policy for a customer I was calling on was that all flights must be booked three weeks in advance for lower airfare. Exceptions must be approved by the company. As I was walking out of a five-day conference in downtown Denver, I was prompted to sit and rest on a bench. By then, I knew that these promptings meant a GUT instinct was forthcoming. I had learned to discipline myself, to submit to promptings like this in order to tune into my GUT instincts and to intentionally manage or tune out all distractions. In so doing, my GUT instincts spoke to me, saying, "Go to Kansas City first thing tomorrow morning."

I thought, "What? Go to Kansas City? I am just coming off of a five-day conference." Then I remembered how much I had been blessed when I tuned out my inner critic and tuned into my GUT instincts. Immediately I sought travel approval, which I did not expect to get since the policy was to book travel three weeks out to get a lower fare. Surprisingly, I got approval to travel if the round-trip flights were under $300.

Southwest Airlines—the LUV airline—to the rescue! I logged onto the Southwest Airlines website. All the fares fitting my itinerary were over $300. Trusting my GUT instincts as I do, I thought, "There is a reason I am to be on that flight tomorrow morning." So I picked up the phone and called customer service. I simply asked if they could help me find an airfare under $300 to Kansas City for tomorrow morning at this late point. The customer service agent clicked on a few reservation screens and said, "You called at exactly the right time. We just had a cancellation, and the fare is only $270." Immediately I booked the flight.

Later that day, I came down with a twenty-four-hour bug. I felt ill, so went to bed, setting my alarm for my early morning flight. Being the daughter of an airline pilot, I have traveled since I was five years old. As a seasoned traveler, I always have at the ready an extra set of clothes, cosmetics, and toiletries that meet current security standards. When the alarm went off at o'dark hundred, I crawled out of bed, threw my jeans and top on, grabbed my prepacked bag, threw my hair in a ponytail, brushed my teeth (you can likely relate—just the basics!) and set out for Denver International Airport. As my parking shuttle approached Southwest Airlines, my GUT instincts softly spoke to me: "Check your bag curbside!"

What? Check my bag curbside? With one exception, I had not checked a travel bag in over twenty years. This was against my travel protocol. Yet, once again, there was my GUT instinct coupled with years of experience in tuning out all external *and* internal distractions and simply listening to, trusting, and acting on my GUT instincts.

As I stepped up to the curbside the baggage claim handler welcomed me and asked me to spell my last name. Slowly I spelled G-R-A-Z-I-A-D-E-I. The following dialogue ensued.

"Oh, yes, I have you and Mike right here!"

"No, it's only me," I said.

"Well, there aren't very many people with the last name and spelling of G-R-A-Z-I-A-D-E-I. Do you know a Mike Graziadei?"

"Well, yes—that is either my ex-husband or my ex-father-in-law."

"Well, look out for him in the seating area because he has a reservation on your flight," said the baggage handler.

I thanked him for the heads-up and expressed that I would first stop in the ladies' room and clean up, since I literally rolled out of bed with no makeup on and certainly wanted to present better than that! He chuckled and said, "Well, this is the LUV airline, you know!"

As we parted ways, he wished me well, and off I went to clean up. After arriving at the departure gate I was so nervous that I sat with my back to the seating area. God was not letting me off the hook; my phone rang. It was a coworker. When I talk business on the phone, I stand up and pace. While discussing business with my colleague, pacing the floor, I looked up and saw my ex-husband, Mike. I said, "Debbie, I have to go. I think I just saw my ex-husband, whom I have not seen in over twenty years."

She was stunned and said, "Go, but call me back as soon as you can."

I barely recognized Mike because, while he looked great (like me), we had both aged over that twenty-year span. As I approached him, I asked, "Excuse me for interrupting you. Are you Mike Graziadei?"

Looking curiously at me, he said, "Yes, I am. You look familiar to me. Where do I know you from?"

I said, "Well, Mike, we were married once."

Our jaws dropped. Long story short, we sat next to one another on the two-and-a-half-hour flight. We talked, we cried, we apologized for our parts in the marriage not working. When the flight landed, we hugged one another and expressed our heartfelt best wishes for each other. All the while, the flight crew was trying to figure out what in the world was going on. After Mike left the plane, I took my seat for the next leg of my flight to Kansas City. The flight crew asked if I was okay. I told them, "More than you know. That was my ex-husband, whom I have not seen in twenty years." They were stunned and exclaimed,

"Well, this is the LUV airline, you know!"

This experience is one of the greatest outcomes that have come to me by practicing Instinctology® as a lifestyle. Had I not tuned into my instincts and disciplined myself to tune out all external and internal distractions, I would have missed the chance of a lifetime to express to this special man my heartfelt sentiments and well wishes. Had I not been a gutsy leader and called Southwest Airlines to seek out a fare under $300, I would have missed this moment of closure that I had long desired.

A Business Instinctology® Success Story—How Listening to, Trusting and Acting on My GUT Instincts Led to Business/Career Success

Time Management and FranklinCovey

Torrey Pines, California, is one of my favorite places to hike. In 1983, Mike and I were forging a cliff with the sea and sun at our back while the trees rustled in the ocean air. Each time I took a breath, I reveled in the moment, taking in its beauty, how good it felt to be outdoors and active. The taste of sea salt on my taste buds made my heart sing.

As we circled a bend on the path, Mike put his hand out to help me up an incline. As I was stepping up, these words were whispered to my spirit, which I now know was God's Utmost Truth guiding and directing me: "You will be teaching time management someday."

As I was a junior in college at San Diego State University, you can imagine that I had some anxiety about my future. This being one of my earliest Instinctology® moments, I casually brushed it off while thinking, "What in the world is time management?" and "How in the world would I become a time management instructor?" This type of job was never mentioned as a career option in any of my college business courses.

Many years later, while living in the San Francisco Bay area, I met someone who was a senior consultant with what was then the Franklin Quest Co., now FranklinCovey. He said to me, "You should teach for Franklin Quest—you would be excellent at it." He then went on to say that the primary course he taught for the company was—wait, hold it…you guessed it!—Values Based Time Management! Stunned, I recalled the words whispered to my sprit in 1983. Immediately, I bought a Franklin Day Planner, began using it daily, and started seeking ways to audition for a senior consultant role with the Franklin Quest Co.

At this time in my life I was a seminar leader with National Seminars Inc., who had sent me to Salt Lake City to deliver a seminar. In the audience was the vice president of human resources for the Franklin Quest Co. Before I had a chance to approach her, she sought me out and invited me to apply and audition for the senior consultant position with her company. Now, keep in mind, at this time, the Franklin Quest Co. had about forty employees and nine or ten senior consultants. When I went for the audition, the other applicants were terrified and anxious. Auditioning to lead Franklin Day Planner seminars was no small feat. Getting such a job would be a turning point in anyone's life. While the other applicants shook in their shoes and spoke of their anxiety prior to entering the audition theater, I was calm and confident. One of them asked me how I could be so calm and confident. I told her my confidence was in the still, small voice that spoke to me years ago in Torrey Pines and that my calm came from trusting the quiet whisper of this internal voice. This has now evolved into my writing and teaching about gutsy leadership and coining and trademarking the word Instinctology®.

I was hired and became a senior consultant for the Franklin Quest Co. in the San Francisco Bay area. This girl was on fire! Now I had gone from being the ashes of a girl in the Midwest who had no confidence to the "It Girl" of the bay area (from ashes to beauty). My extended biological family was blown away, for mostly all they had ever done was criticize and put me down.

So, how did I go from being in the pit like Joseph to an acclaimed speaker and spokesperson in a major market? The only answer is that years earlier, in 1983, I listened to, trusted, and acted on my GUT instincts, God's Utmost Truth within me, which overrode negative internal scripts and beliefs as well as negativity from outsiders telling me that I was too young for this position. Franklin Quest's vice president of HR had invited me to apply and audition, yet told me that the competition was fierce and the audition tactics the company used tested a presenter's ability to focus. And finally, a gap in my beliefs and values made it hard for me to accept and receive this great opportunity that put me on the path to my destiny. This job tripled my income, which allowed me to buy a home and settle in the bay area. This is where I lived and thrived for many years. While I love Colorado and Kansas, you might say that I left my heart in San Francisco.

Are you seeing the correlation of Instinctology® being a tool to help you be a Gutsy Leader? To get the results you want? To make a difference in your life? To turn your GUT instincts into concrete action? Finally, to bridge your three gaps? The key is that you must learn to listen to, trust, and act on your GUT instincts. I will teach you how to do this through the acronym ACT in Section II of this book.

Meanwhile, the story does not end here. Recently I had the good fortune to reconnect with my friend and mentor Hyrum Smith, Co-founder/former CEO of FranklinCovey. It turns out that our present-day work is quite complimentary. We both still want to make a difference in the world. He is doing so with his teaching and new book *The 3 Gaps*. I am doing so with my teaching and my own new book *Instinctology®: A Leadership Method to Turn GUT Instincts into Concrete Action*.

A Service to Others Success Story—How Listening to, Trusting and Acting on My GUT Instincts Led to Serving Others in Need

The Colorado Housing Crisis of 2015

Building on the prior story, two major events have happened in my life since moving to Colorado. Both of them have given me the opportunity to serve people in need that I deeply care about.

Denver has recently experienced a housing crisis. While there is a positive side to the escalating real estate market, there is also a negative side. Higher home prices have resulted in rental fees that have double or tripled, displacing many hardworking, responsible, good, and honest people from their homes. The nightly local news is deluged with stories about hardworking and responsible individuals who have been displaced from their homes due to rental fees escalating overnight by up to 30 percent, far beyond standard annual income increases. There is a two-year waiting list for homeless shelters and for available income assisted housing. By the hoards, people are moving in with family and friends or living out of their cars in Walmart parking lots.

One such situation is my friend of forty-plus years who works in the public schools. She also has a twelve-year-old son. This friend happened to live about five miles from me when this housing crisis hit the greater Denver area. Her daughter called me and told me what was going on, and that my dear friend was one of the 10,000 people in Denver facing this overnight crisis.

My GUT instincts had instructed me to buy a home when I moved to Colorado, prior to the price hike. This now became a home for not only me, but also for my lifelong friend and her son. Tuning into, trusting, and acting on your GUT instincts will always be for not only your highest good, but also for the highest good of others!

My beloved Aunt Jana Kay in Wyoming

Trusting my GUT instincts has also resulted in service to my Aunt Jana. Since my move to Colorado, my Aunt Jana, who means everything to me, has fallen ill with dementia. She and my uncle live in Cody, Wyoming, which is only a one-hour, fifteen-minute flight from Denver. Being able to easily access Wyoming and visit my family frequently has allowed me to help my uncle as he cares daily for my aunt. It has also given me the joy of spending quality time with Jana, serving and showering her with love and gratitude for how she has always been there for me and others. We can enjoy one another's company while she still knows who I am. This book is dedicated to Jana.

In all of my life, I have never felt so aligned with my destiny and service to others. This is truly one of the greatest rewards of tuning into, trusting, and acting on your GUT instincts. The feeling of inner peace from being in the middle of God's will in service to others is one of the greatest satisfactions I have ever known. I guess Mick Jagger needs Instinctology®, since he "Can't Get No Satisfaction"! These are amazing stories, and there's more! Read on…

A Personal Enjoyment Success Story—How Listening to, Trusting and Acting on My Gut Instincts Has Brought Me Joy and Enriched My Life

Santorini View Serigraph by Artist Howard Behrens

In the summer of 1979, my dear friend for more than forty years now, Mary, and I backpacked Europe. We lived on fine European breads, cheeses, and wines while traversing Europe and Ireland. Many an adventure was had! The best of them came when, toward the end of our trip, we were running out of funds. We stayed three weeks on the Greek island of Santorini. We saved money on train rides, food, and youth hostels by sleeping in our sleeping bags on the beach, being fed by the locals, and hiking the five-mile island perimeter daily. This was long before Santorini became the expensive and popular vacation spot that you now see highlighted on American Express commercials. The locals fed us, watched over us, and gave us safe refuge, allowing us to enjoy the sun, sand, and ouzo without spending a penny for the three weeks we explored their beautiful island.

One day, we hiked up the hill and discovered what the locals believe is the lost city of Atlantis. The next day, we hiked farther, to the top of the town of Fira, where we sat for hours taking in the blue hues of the ocean and pastel shades of the village, saturating ourselves with sun and breathing the clear sea breeze. Rather than describing this scene to you, I'll let you enjoy this painting of us lounging on the steps of Fira on this gorgeous island. Unbeknownst to Mary or me, the man that we saw behind us sketching that day was sketching us. That sketch, along with his creativity and talent, later became this painting.

It is Instinctology® that led me to discover this painting, which my then-husband bought for me. This painting is hanging in my home to this day. Living in the San Francisco Bay area was a dream come true for me. Mike and I loved all of the outdoor activities that we could do together there, like walking the hills or riding the streetcars of San Francisco. We would enjoy this outing on weekends, starting at the wharf and working our way back to Ghirardelli Square. One day, my GUT instinct switched up our direction by whispering to me, "Start your walk at Ghirardelli Square this time."

And so we did. In so doing, we walked a different route that took us down the streets to the heart of the art district. As we walked along, gazing into the gallery windows, we came to the Howard Behrens gallery window, in which the above painting was prominently displayed.

Stunned, I stopped and stared. Mike kept walking for a moment and then turned around and asked me why I had stopped walking. Speechless, I motioned to him to come see the painting in the window called *Santorini View*. Together we stood frozen in time, trying to make sense of how Mary and I were in the painting of the exact spot where we had lounged in Santorini years ago.

We spoke to the art dealer, who contacted Howard Behrens's office and then told us that, in fact, the painting was based on a sketch of two women in Santorini, sitting at the top of the Fira town stairs in the summer of 1979.

Not only did my European backpacking trip and time in Santorini enrich my life and provide soulful memories, it also produced this treasured painting that now hangs in my living room. It brings me joy and artistic pleasure every time I look at it. I would have missed this great joy had I not listened to, trusted, and acted on my GUT instincts that told me to switch up the direction for that weekend's San Francisco's city/wharf walk.

A Spiritual/Physical Health Success Story—How Listening to, Trusting and Acting on My GUT Instincts Led to Improved Spirituality and Physical Health

There is a phone call one never wants to receive. For me, it was the call that my little brother, Miles, had been struck by a drunk driver and died on impact. I refused to believe the caller. While driving to the hospital, I was in complete denial. However, when the doctor walked toward me in the emergency room foyer, I saw in his face that it was true. My best friend and brother had left this earth at the young age of twenty-four.

My body in shock, I collapsed to the floor and woke up to my grandmother watching over me. I was filled with prescription drugs to treat the trauma of shock to the body. I was only twenty-seven years old and had always enjoyed excellent health. However, after losing Miles, I rarely ate or exercised, and I went into a deep depression. My marriage helped me to move on. Then, some years later, my mom passed at the early age of sixty-four. Between the two losses, I almost completely stopped functioning and definitely was suffering emotionally and physically.

On a weekend trip to Napa Valley, my GUT instincts directed me to go to the airshow across the street from Wilkinson's bed and breakfast, where I was staying.

I did not want to go, since there were crowds of people that I did not wish to get caught up in. However, by now I was growing in my confidence to trust and act on my GUT instincts, so I went. I recall the emotional and physical pain of missing Miles and Mom. Of course, my beliefs were that they were in heaven and surrounded by light and love. Flooded by the pain of loss, I fell to the temptation of doubt and began to wonder if they were okay. I should share that the reason I would go to Napa Valley was because my health was deteriorating. The spring-fed mineral baths and mud baths of Calistoga fueled my body and restored my strength. I also needed my spirit and faith in God to be renewed.

While I was standing in the crowd at the airshow, a man standing next to me spoke to me. I looked up at him. He was tall, tanned, and strikingly handsome. He and I were pinned in together. The people crowded around us were huddled up like penguins seeking warmth and survival from an Antarctic snowstorm with seventy-mile-per-hour winds and forty degrees below zero temperatures. Like a penguin in the middle of their huddle, one simply could not move in this crowd of people at the airshow. As I looked up at the man, he said these words: "Miles is okay. Your mom is okay. You need to release them so that you can be okay."

"Huh? What?" I exclaimed and turned my head away in disbelief for only a few seconds. When I turned back, this man was gone.

Now, this may be hard for you to believe. You simply have to trust me. There was nowhere for him to go. The crowd was both dense and tight. To this day, I believe that he was an angel visiting this heartbroken woman who, having lost her two closest loved ones, was becoming lost herself.

This angel's visit left me with an energy that surged through my body. In that moment, I felt physically hungry for the first time in months. Later, while I ate a full meal, I noticed that for the first time since both losses my all-consuming grief had been replaced with an aura of peace. This angelic visit was also the beginning of my faith in God being renewed. I still had a long way to go on both counts. However, this touch by an angel gave me the impetus that I needed to move forward.

In Latin, *graziadei* means "thanks be to God." Thanks be to God that I had learned by then to listen to, trust, and act on my GUT instincts. On this day, my GUT told me to walk into the middle of the crowd at the airshow across the street from my Calistoga bed and breakfast on my weekend getaway.

When people show you who they are, believe them.
—MAYA ANGELOU

Darkness wants to consume your light.
Don't let it. Let your light shine!
—ROBEN GRAZIADEI

Gutsy, instinctual leaders see beyond the
ordinary to the extraordinary…
Beyond the visible to the invisible,
Beyond the possible to the impossible,
Beyond the risk to the benefits,
Beyond their wants to other's needs,
Beyond failure to failing forward,
Beyond following others to leading
with their GUT instincts.
—LARRY KEEFAUVER

Darkness cannot consume the light.
That is why there are stars in the sky.
—ROBEN GRAZIADEI

The Author's Instinctology® Failing Forward Story

Heretofore, I have shared with you Instinctology® success stories that led to increased inner peace, spiritual abundance, healed relationships, service to others, personal enjoyment, and improved physical health. The reality is that I am human and make mistakes. Though I write and teach Instinctology®, like you I sometimes fail at listening to, trusting in, and acting on my GUT instincts. The following is a story full of invaluable lessons that I learned from *not* turning my GUT instincts into concrete action.

An Instinctology® Failing Forward Story—How Ignoring My GUT Instincts Gave Me the Opportunity to Learn and Fail Forward

While I have become proficient at leading an Instinctology® lifestyle, I am human and make mistakes. One such mistake nearly took me out completely as a result of blatantly ignoring an instinct so strong that the hair on the back of my neck stood up and I felt chills down my spine as the cold surrounded me.

All of the accounts that I have shared with you thus far are success stories—stories of great outcomes and service to others due to leading by my GUT instincts as defined as listening to, trusting, and acting on them. These real-life accounts are evidence of how I have become a better business, community, and family leader by making Instinctology® my lifestyle.

From my days of teaching Kouzes's and Posner's *The Leadership Challenge* adventure courses for the Tom Peters Group Learning Systems, I knew well the principal of "failing forward." I recall thinking after I had crashed and burned, "Okay, I failed at honoring my GUT instincts, which are always for the highest good of myself and others. Yet all is not lost. I can learn from this and fail forward."

Here is my Instinctology® failing forward story, which ultimately has taught me invaluable lessons that I now apply as a gutsy leader, turning my GUT instincts into concrete action. You can fail forward too, and if that sounds counterintuitive to you…that's OK. Hopefully this story will shed some light on Kouzes's and Posner's concept of failing forward.

From Ashes to Beauty

In October 2013, while walking on the beautiful Country Club Plaza of Kansas City, Missouri, my GUT instincts led me to coin and trademark the word Instinctology®. The ultimate result of turning that GUT instinct into concrete action is the book you now hold in your hands and the workshops that our Instinctologists® teach. Suddenly, my life course had changed. My focus became the writing of this book, building an Internet platform, and trademarking/branding Instinctology®. This girl was on fire again! This time around, she had founded a new lifestyle brand, Instinctology®, and was embarking on the exciting journey of teaching and writing about the study and habit of turning your GUT instincts into concrete action.

Around this same time, I met a man through an online dating site. I ended up going on a first date with him in November 2013. I will spare you the details. But to convey why it will go down in history as one of the worst first dates ever, I will share with you that he spent the entire dinner telling me his sad story about every woman who had left him and how he was afraid I would leave him once I knew the truth about him. I took the bait hook, line, and sinker. I felt so sad for him that as much as my GUT instincts told me to run, I allowed my compassion to override my instincts. This misstep led to a temporary downward spiral in my life and delayed my Instinctology® project.

I was never one to run out on a date, but on this occasion I really wanted to jump ship. While sitting across the table from him as he spoke, the hair on the back of my neck stood up and a visceral chill ran down my spine. This time, not only did my GUT instincts tell me to run, but my body also spoke volumes of Instinctology® to me. Against my better judgment, my body, and my GUT instincts telling to me to "run", I allowed the internal distraction and sense of obligation (don't run out on a date) as well as my sympathy for this man's pain to override my impeccable instincts. I failed to manage an internal script/distraction as well as the external distractions (a lively restaurant and a glass of wine). I ignored my GUT instincts that were speaking quite loudly to me. My life-giving GUT instincts were giving me invaluable information. If I had led from my GUT, I would have saved myself a lot of unnecessary pain. I allowed the internal scripts in my mind to trump my invaluable and impeccable GUT instincts. My brain began presenting reasonable logic (otherwise known in our Western culture as data) that I allowed to trump my GUT instincts. In so doing, I learned some of the greatest Instinctology® lessons, which have now become some of the richest content for my work around Instinctology®. Because I had allowed myself to be manipulated and subsequently ignored my GUT instincts, this book was put on hold for about a year while trying to break free of the nightmare that entangled my life and placed me on a temporary reactive downward spiral.

The lesson I learned from this "failing forward" story is to remember that some relationships can be devastated by the cancers of domination, intimidation, and manipulation. Neither he nor I were leading from our GUT instincts, but rather from internal scripts and external forces that sought to squelch God's Utmost Truth within us and God's highest good for all. I am thankful to my amazing girlfriends and my family, who stood by me and constantly reminded me to trust my GUT instinct, that still small voice within me, over anything and everything else. By listening to, trusting, and acting on my God-given, empowering gift of GUT instincts, I found the strength to completely break away from this negative and destructive situation that life had presented to me. Not only did I survive—I was able to rise above the circumstances, thriving and like the Phoenix, rise out of the ashes. Hence the name of this Instinctology® story, "From Ashes to Beauty."

In the process of failing forward, a concept that can serve you well too, I learned indispensable lessons that have strengthened my Instinctology® resolve. With Instinctology® resolute in my being, it was a cinch to harness its power during my ten days in the ICU (dodged a bullet story) that I shared with you earlier. I am grateful! For not only did I learn invaluable lessons and fail forward; with a deeper depth and breadth, I have written and published *Instinctology®: A Leadership Method to Turn GUT Instincts into Concrete Action.* It is my hope that these stories will encourage you to lead from your GUT instincts for the highest good of yourself and others.

Let's now unpack the acronym GUT.

SECTION II

Great leaders create a culture where it is safe
to take risk, make mistakes, and fail forward.
—Barry Posner

That which is to give light must endure burning.
—Victor Frankel

If you don't know where you're going,
any road will get you there.
—Alice in Wonderland

As a leader, pushing yourself is a requirement to
grow and develop. You must gather the strength
and fortitude to take calculated risks when your
instincts tell you it's time to take action in your
efforts to anticipate the unexpected. How will you
ever know what you are capable of (or not) unless
you take on the added responsibility that forces you
to step up your game? As you learn to trust your
gut along the way, soon other people will too.
—Glenn Llopis in *Forbes*[4]

---

4 http://www.forbes.com/sites/glennllopis/2015/01/26/5-reasons-leaders-have-trouble-trustin
gtheirinstincts/2/#2ab6517f6470

CHAPTER 3

The Acronym GUT Explained

et us now take a deeper dive into understanding what our GUT instincts are, where they come from, and how they can empower us to lead more effectively, love more fully, and live more abundantly.

As a motivational speaker, trainer and management consultant, I have taught that GUT Instincts are:

- **G**od's—your higher power
- **U**tmost—the highest good for yourself and others
- **T**ruth—within you, leading from the inside out

I am convinced that listening to, trusting, and acting on your GUT instincts is the key to freedom from suffering and movement toward personal empowerment and prosperity. Personally I have come to enjoy improved relationships, a deeper spirituality, more fulfilling work, and increase in my health and wealth by leading from my GUT Instincts.

To expound on this conviction, permit me to briefly define each word in GUT—<u>**G**od's **U**tmost **T**ruth.</u>

God's

- **God is the higher power**—omnipotent, if you will. This belief in a higher power is often cited in twelve-step recovery and rehab programs. For me, I recognize that I am powerless to make life-giving decisions without God, this higher power from my Creator. This power grounds me—the grounding of my being helps me connect to myself and to love myself in a healthy way so that I can selflessly love others while staying empowered by my GUT instincts. Because I am grounded in a higher power, I don't have to exercise power or be empowered and thus enslaved by stuff, others, or magic. I am free to choose service to others instead self-aggrandizing decisions that prosper and profit me at the expense of others. I am in business, in sales, and in the corporate world. I need this higher power to correct, discipline, and balance out my self-seeking power to survive, make a profit, and win in business. This higher power helps to ground me in ethical and moral decisions. Win-win scenarios are when the client or customer is served while also realizing that doing the right thing leads to right outcomes for a company, their customers, and employees. I am not all-powerful, all-knowing, or all-present (i.e., I am not God), which leads us to the next core belief that many of us share about God.

- **God is the Creator.** I did not make me. Furthermore, I do not have the wisdom to keep me alive and from dying. Shocker? Not really. You probably believe something very close to that yourself. Having confessed that I am not the inventor of me helps me step away from pride and arrogance while treating others with dignity and respect, as I believe we are all created in the image of God. Simply put, there is some of the nature of the Divine, that still, small voice and inner wisdom deposited in each of us. A sense of purpose, self-awareness, and ability to care for others mentality rises above base instincts of survival, to win at all costs, and a me-first at the expense of other's well-being.

- **Your higher power is wisdom and truth.** Yes, there's something beyond or transcendent to human knowledge and intellect. Mind researchers talk about God genes and DNA in us that are hard-wired into our brains. Philosophers, professors, and ethicists write about morality, the good, servant leadership, and doing unto others as we would have others do unto us.

- **Your higher power guides your conscience.** Though we often meet people who appear to have a seared conscience—completely cut off from their GUT instincts, God's Utmost Truth within them—society acknowledges that all humans do have a conscience. This conscience keeps us individually and collectively from total self-depredation and global destruction. Wise people from the ancient past to the modern day have recognized the existence of a moral compass or guide within us called our conscience. The following are a few examples:

From America's founders to our present-day Supreme Court justices, our country's government leaders, lawyers, writers, philosophers, educators, theologians, business leaders, motivational speakers, benefactors, philanthropists, coaches, etc. all have made references to conscience, making morally right decisions, serving the common good, and being of service to others. One writer talks about our "heart-mind" (*nous* in Greek) or soul being like a radio tuned into a moral whisper.

What is reality? Is it the "bag of goods" reality television sells us? Or is it the no-spin message of your GUT instincts, which are the gifts that keep on giving that you must unwrap for yourself? No one else can open this gift for you or take it from you. Like Victor Frankl, whom I quoted earlier, no one can take away from you your right to lead from your GUT instincts.

He that loses his conscience has nothing
left that is worth keeping.
—Caution, c. 1645, The Holy Court

Trust that man in nothing who has
not a conscience in everything.
—Laurence Sterne, 1713–68,
Tristram Shandy, bk 17

I cannot and will not cut my conscience
to fit this year's fashion.
—Lillian Hellman, 1905–84, Letter to the
House Committee on Un-American Activities

Conscience is a soft whisper of the God in man.
—Edward Young

Utmost

Utmost may be defined as final, complete, whole, finished, ultimate, as well as highest and best. One bestselling writer named Oswald Chambers had his inspirational talks to his workers in Egypt posthumously pulled together by his wife in perhaps the bestselling daily devotional of all time, *My Utmost for His Highest.*

When referring to what's utmost, our GUT instincts push us toward excellence, the greater and highest good, the best results and outcomes for others and ourselves in business, family, religion, politics, morality, ethics, and decision making. What's ultimate is what's final or *telos* (Greek: complete, finished, and perfected). Our GUT instincts help us finish what we start. At times, we want to procrastinate or not decide when a right decision is begging both our attention and our resolution. We need to focus, to fight, and to finish strong and right. Our GUT instincts help us to run the race and to win with excellence for the *utmost* and highest good of all.

Utmost refers to ideas from our GUT instincts, God's Utmost Truth within us allowing us to lead from the inside out. As I shared with you earlier, the word Instinctology® was provided to me through my GUT instincts. GUT instinct ideas are rooted in the Creator's nature—innovative, creative, leading edge, right, merciful, loving, kind, and just, to name a few. Such are the virtues of conscience that Secretary of Education Bill Richardson wrote about in *The Book of Virtues*—self-discipline, compassion, responsibility, friendship, work, courage, perseverance, honesty, loyalty, and faith. Ultimate decisions are marked by these virtues and are rooted in truth—not just *a* truth, but ultimate or absolute truth. Let us now examine the "truth" of truth.

Truth

Truth in Hebrew thought *(amet)* refers to any complete consistency between one's inner and outer life. What one does and says are fully congruent with who one is. The inner and outer selves line up. Abraham Maslow refers to this as "self-actualization." Modern language references this as "walking your talk." Kouzes and Posner, authors of *The Leadership Challenge*, refer to this as "doing what you say you will do," also known as DWYSYWD. Hyrum Smith, inventor of the Franklin Day Planner, refers to this as inner peace. Tom Peters, a guru of management consulting and author of *In Search of Excellence*, might think of this as the pursuit of excellence. Ken Blanchard, a leadership expert, might exclaim that if you want to be an effective one-minute manager, consider your GUT instincts as part of the management equation.

Our GUT instincts come out of integrity—integer is one, i.e. unity. My GUT instincts guide me along a consistent path of making pure, right, and just decisions that bring the highest good into the lives of both others and myself. Others can rely on me to speak the truth in love to them and with an honest examination of my heart about myself. We are honest and consistent. Promises are kept, and contracts are fulfilled. Thoughts are positive and affirming instead of being critical, judgmental, and negative. Actions are win-win and "all-serving" instead of self-centered and self-serving.

We may think that human reason is ultimate truth. From the enlightened elite, our Western mind-sets have pushed us in this direction. As mentioned earlier, we are trained in binary code thinking—yes or no, on or off, black or white, yin or yang. In other cultures, the abstract is embraced and even referred to as a greater wisdom than binary thinking.

The way to find truth, Descartes said, was to strip the mind of everything that can possibly be doubted until we finally reach a bedrock of truths that cannot possibly be doubted. He believed that he himself had dug deep enough to hit that infallible bedrock in his famous cogito: "I think, therefore I am." After all, even when we are doubting everything, we are still thinking, and therefore the surest thing we can know is the existence of the thinking subject. The idea emerged that by a method of systematic doubt, the human mind—or Reason (often capitalized)—could attain godlike objectivity and certainty. In one of my college philosophy courses, the professor liked to define objectivity as "the way God sees things." Though not a believer in God as a higher power, his point was that true objectivity could be attained only by a *being* who transcends this world and knows everything as it truly is.

The hubris of the Enlightenment lay in thinking that Reason was just such a transcendent power, providing infallible knowledge. Reason became nothing less than an idol, taking the place of God as the source of absolute truth. Ironically, Descartes himself was a devout Catholic; he was so certain that God had revealed to him the irrefutable logic of the cogito that he vowed to make a pilgrimage to the shrine of Our Lady of Loreto in Italy—which he did a few years later. Descartes helped to establish a form of rationalism that treated Reason not merely as the human ability to think rationally, but as an infallible and autonomous source of truth. Reason came to be seen as a storehouse of truths independent of any religion or philosophy.[5]

As a believer in Christ and his lifestyle, I often refer to Jesus, like many do, as a humble servant. Dare I say that he led by his GUT instincts? While he was willing to lay down his life for others as a friend, Jesus also had boundaries, as evidenced by the times he retreated for rest and solitude. At times, his highest good for others required him to be still, rest, and refresh. This boundary today is missing in many of our busy lives. Yet this process is required in order to practice Instinctology® as a life-giving leadership approach and lifestyle.

---

5 Pearce, Nancy. *Total Truth: Liberating Christianity from Its Cultural Captivity*. Good News Publishers/Crossway Books. Kindle Edition. Kindle Locations 911-924.

With the aforementioned definitions of Instinctology® and GUT instincts in mind, let's dive into ACT: how to lead from your GUT instincts.

Why Might We Resist Leading from Our GUT Instincts?

Let's first examine why we are prone to resist leading from our GUT instincts. At the beginning of this chapter, I shared a quote from Glenn Llopis's article in *Forbes* titled "Five Reasons Leaders Have Trouble Trusting Their Instincts." See if any of his list coincides with the reason(s) you have difficulty trusting your GUT instincts. (I have listed the issues he identified with my comments.)

1. **Unfavorable Outcomes:** You second-guess your GUT because you have experienced disappointing results. You think that you trusted your GUT in the past and it didn't work out to your satisfaction.
2. **Fear of Uncertainty:** Leading from a focal point of fear will always distort both your core values and your ability to make right choices.
3. **Can't Deliver:** Perhaps in the past, when you trusted your GUT, you overpromised yourself and others but underperformed. Or maybe you have a perfectionist streak in you. You expect perfection from yourself rather than pursing excellence. There is a big difference!
4. **Dictates of the Marketplace:** When your instincts go against conventional wisdom, pleasing others, or workplace limitations, you default to conventional wisdom or pundits instead of standing up, moving forward, and making a difference.
5. **Clouded Judgment:** A double-minded leader who cannot trust his or her GUT will be unstable in every way.[6] Let's return to my "swing the bat" analogy. Stan Musial is quoted

---

6 James 1:2–8

as saying, "A lot of hitters stay away from the plate; some are close up, some are forward, some are back. The thing about hitting is this: You have to know the strike zone. Hit strikes and put the ball on the bat."[7] Perhaps the greatest hitter of all time was focused on hitting. He trusted his gut on swinging at strikes and connecting the bat with the ball. His judgment was clear. He wasn't at the plate to swing at just anything or not to swing at all. A gutsy leader has clear, focused, truth-based, sound judgment.

Are you accountable enough for your actions as a leader? Do you feel compelled to prove others wrong when they don't buy into the nontraditional path your instincts are telling you to take? Oftentimes leaders don't trust their instincts (even though they know it's the right thing to do) because they don't know if they can sell their ideas and points of view to their colleagues and see matters all the way through to the end.

Let's turn now to the acronym ACT, whereby I will teach you how to turn your gut instincts into concrete action.

---

7 http://www.brainyquote.com/quotes/quotes/s/stanmusial532481.html

Nothing can dim the light that
shines from within you.
—**Maya Angelou**

Knowing yourself is the beginning of all wisdom.
—**Aristotle**

My greatest accomplishment was to stay
true to who I am in a world where so
many were pressuring me not to.
—**Albert Einstein**

Everything can be taken from a man but one
thing: the last of the human freedoms -
to choose one's attitude in any given set of
circumstances, to choose one's way.
—**Viktor E. Frankl**

No one can take away from you your right to
choose to lead from your GUT instincts.
—**Roben Graziadei**

CHAPTER 4

ACT: How to Turn Your GUT Instincts into Concrete Action

Introduction

Given twenty-first-century technology and our learned resistance to leading from our GUT instincts, we need tools to train ourselves on how to lead from our GUT instincts. You can masterfully change your life and get the positive results that you want with the highest good for yourself and others in mind. Using the acronym ACT, I will teach you three tools that will empower you to practice Instinctology®, Life-giving Leadership from Your GUT as a lifestyle.

- **A = Authenticity (being true to GUT instincts/self)**
- **C = Conscious choice/intention**
- **T = Turning GUT instincts into action**

A= Authenticity GUT Instinct   C =Conscious Choice/Intention   T= Turn Instinct into Action

I love studying the life of Albert Einstein. In one of his biographies, he spoke of what he considered his greatest accomplishment. It was not discovering E=MC². It was knowing who he was purposed to be and staying true to this. In fact, Albert Einstein is said to have gone into a deep depression when he realized that the nuclear energy formula he discovered and imagined bringing peace to the planet instead would be used for just the opposite effect—war and destruction. Einstein knew who he was, a man of peace. Some wanted to use his talents for things that he did not desire to happen. Staying true to himself was what he deemed to be his greatest accomplishment; in doing so, he became a gutsy leader.

Viktor Frankl knew who he was and what he believed, and he held to those beliefs under the most horrendous circumstances that one could imagine. Held captive in a Nazi concentration camp for many years after being stripped of his home, family, and health, he stuck to his convictions. He lifted himself and others by encouraging prisoners to hold strong to their beliefs, for your beliefs are a human right that cannot be taken from you. Beaten and starved while sleeping in lice- and rat-infested barracks with temperatures sometimes below zero, dressed in tattered clothing, having no shoes, this man clung to the last of his human rights—the right to stand firm on his beliefs and attitudes.

Could he have done this if he was not confident in what he believed? If he was internally conflicted as to his faith, beliefs, core values, guiding principles, and chosen attitude? I think not. It is in our times of greatest suffering that our true beliefs are tested and brought to the surface. He mastered knowing who he was now and who he was becoming.

A = AUTHENTICITY

The first step to becoming authentic is to examine yourself and to honestly identify any internal *core* beliefs that are not in concert with your daily behaviors. Ask yourself this key question:

Does what I verbally claim to believe mirror my external actions and behaviors?

Be brave and ask those that you trust and know you well:

What, if any, gaps between your expressed beliefs and daily actions do they perceive in you?

Like me, you too might have an "aha" moment that leads to a huge paradigm shift. I highly recommend that you read Hyrum Smith's best-selling book *The 3 Gaps.* Closing your belief gaps is the most dynamic, personal, and life-changing work that you can do for yourself and others. You will experience inner peace and empowerment like never before. Your beliefs determine your thoughts, which shape your feelings and drive your actions. Conflicting core beliefs and actions result in a lack of authenticity. This lack of authenticity blocks your ability to tune into your GUT instincts and listen to them clearly. Learning to trust and act on them empowers you to lead from your GUT.

Recall the "failing forward" story that I shared with you in Section I of this book. This life experience led me to examine myself with specific regard to my core beliefs like never before. The resulting outcome was that, like the phoenix rising out of the ashes, I am now stronger, clearer, and more confident in one of my core beliefs than ever before in my life. The clarity that has come from this paradigm shift has propelled me forward (failing forward) in my life. At the same time, I also saw God as loving, creative, all-powerful, and having no darkness in him, only light. You see, my belief gap was ultimately about who and what image I was created in. I had not yet clearly and firmly decided which religious teaching of God I *agreed* with. This internal conflict has been put to rest. From this belief gap stemmed an external situation in my life that mirrored my internal conflicted beliefs about who I was. Was I created in the image of a hellfire-and-brimstone

God, or was I created in the image of a loving, creative, powerful, energizing and life-giving God of light?

As you have most likely guessed by now, I came out of this tornado with a firmly committed belief that I was created in the image of a loving God. If I am created in the image of a loving God, should I not be leading the productive life I was created for?

Candidly speaking, each of us, including the persons in my "failing forward" story, can learn to lead from our GUT instincts with the highest good of ourselves and others at heart. If we are willing to take this journey of self-examination related to our core beliefs and actions being in alignment, we can actualize our authenticity, clearing the way to listen to, trust, and act on our GUT instincts, leading ourselves from the inside out.

If you believe, you can achieve—that's my motto!
—SOPHIE TURNER

He that would have fruit must climb the tree.
—THOMAS FULLER

Your intuition knows what to write,
so get out of the way.
—RAY BRADBURY

What you believe with 100 percent clarity
becomes your actualized authenticity.
—ROBEN GRAZIADEI

Ask yourself these questions. Write your answers down. A person's retention of material increases by 87 percent when that person takes notes. Take notes here in the book or in your own journal. Take some quality time for yourself in order to answer these questions. You, your loved ones, and all those that you lead are worth you taking this time.

Remember your wheel with the spokes representing parts of your life?

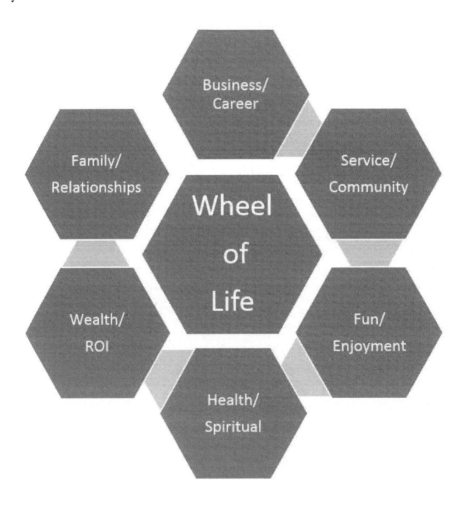

Ask yourself…

- What is working in your life right now?
- What in your life is not working to your satisfaction right now?
- With which spoke are you getting the results that you want in your life and leadership endeavors?
- With which spoke are you not getting the results that you want?

Example: I was getting the results that I wanted in my life financially, spiritually, and professionally.

Example: I was not getting the results that I wanted in seeking to be in a healthy relationship with a life-giving person.

In answering these and other questions that I share in my workshops and coaching, I discovered that I needed to do some work to close one of my core belief gaps. Once I did so, I had the resolve I needed and internal fortitude to go back to the beginning, that first date, when my GUT instinct said, "Run!" With this firmly rooted core belief clarified, I was able to actualize my authentic self and take a stand for my GUT instinct, which said, "No, this is not the person that I want to be with!" In the face of religious legalism, social norms and pressures, and ineffective internal scripts, I was able to practice Instinctology®, life-giving leadership from my GUT! From my GUT instincts, I led myself first. Then I became able to lead others from my experiences, all the while listening to what truly was for the highest good of both myself and others, yielding the optimum outcomes that I wanted:

1) To be free of a couple of unhealthy persons in my life.
2) To open the door and hold the space for future healthy relationships in my life.

Suffice it to say that I am much happier now. I am leading more effectively from my GUT instincts for the good of myself and others in both my personal and business leadership endeavors. This lays the foundation and takes us to the letter C in the word ACT. C stands for Conscious Choice and Intention.

Confidence is something you create within
yourself by believing in who you are.
—UNKNOWN

Nobody can make you feel inferior
without your consent.
—ELEANOR ROOSEVELT

It's not who you are that holds you back.
It's who you think you're not.
—ERIC THOMAS

My self-esteem is high because I honor who I am.
—LOUISE HAY

Second-guessing yourself means you lack confidence.
Lacking confidence means you have no faith,
and no faith equals failure. No time for that.
—NANA ZARA

Go confidently in the direction of your dream.
—MAX EHRMANN

C = Conscious Choice & Intention

With the letter A, you actualized your authentic self. Now you are primed to take charge of the reactive cycles in your life and turn them into proactive/productive life cycles. The tool that I will teach you to help you do this is something I call the "Confidence and Creation Cycle." Having worked with thousands individually and in groups, I found two patterns consistently emerged for both myself and others.

The first pattern was this: As an individual took their first step of confidence to create or produce an outcome he or she sought, his or her confidence grew even when they did not get the outcome they anticipated. Consequently, this new level of confidence led to more creativity, which eventually resulted in the person's intended outcomes. In turn, this fueled optimism and created a proactive/productive life cycle, a "Confidence and Creation Cycle", tailored specifically to that person!

Confidence leads to creativity.
Creativity leads to confidence,
Propelling you forward with
life-giving and productive life cycles.

Thus your "Confidence and Creation Cycle," tailored to your unique DNA, is birthed.

The second pattern was this: Life with its hard knocks and unexpected losses/surprises had worn many people down, resulting in unwanted outcomes of living reactively and not being in control of their lives. People need support in turning this reactivity into proactivity. The only way to break a habit or to turn negative reactivity into positive proactivity is to replace our response with more productive thoughts, feelings, and actions. I get that these two words—reactive and proactive—have become societal buzzwords, which tend to lose their clout after a while. Yet, their precise meanings are the groundwork for building a confidence and creation cycle tailored to you.

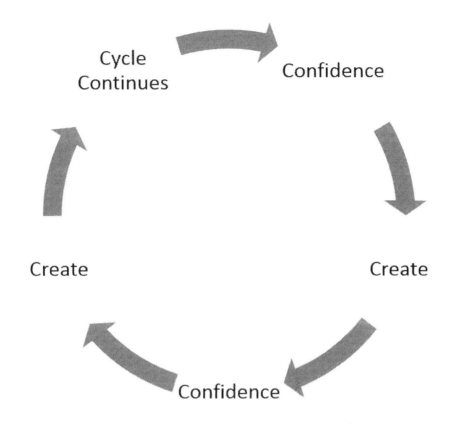

Cycle
Continues

Confidence

Create

Create

Confidence

Reactivity means acting in response to a situation rather than creating or controlling it.

Proactivity means to create or control a situation by causing something to happen, rather than responding to it after it has happened.

Consider your life or the lives of those around you. Few people are confidently living a proactive life and getting the positive results that they want. Now contemplate the inverse. How many people do you know who are living a reactive life, chasing something that has no true meaning for them, running in the rat race of life and wearing out their treadmills? It seems as if reactive cycles are controlling us instead of our being in control of the proactive cycles in our lives.

How does that happen? Recently, I decided to stop watching violent, dark movies and television programming. Remember the cliché "garbage in, garbage out"? Instead, I now view uplifting programming that deposits positive thoughts, feelings, and actions into my mind. This is what the "Confidence and Creation Cycle" can do for you. Technology in general can also rob you of your time and block your ability to tune into your GUT instincts. The "Confidence and Creation Cycle" can help you tune out of technology and tune inward, thus leading yourself and others from the inside out.

As I taught this tool for many years, it came in handy for me. Please recall the success stories that I shared with you. The financial increase that resulted from real estate transactions illustrates how the "Confidence and Creation Cycle" can help you move from reactivity to proactivity, stick to your guns, be a gutsy leader, and get the optimum results that you want. Let's unpack this:

- It took an initial step of confidence for me to ask a Realtor to list my property for sale at the price I asked. Many naysayers refused to do so; some even mocked me.
- This first step of confidence, even though I did not immediately get the outcome I wanted, inspired me to become creative about how I would find a Realtor to list this property at the price I was asking. I had to come up with a creative approach. Asking around, I found a hungry Realtor who was willing to give it a go.
- This led to more confidence for both me and the Realtor, which prompted us to brainstorm creative avenues for marketing my property. Together we decided to list the property in the *San Francisco Chronicle* with a reach to San Francisco proper (six hours from upper northern California, where my property for sale was located). That listing brought us the buyer who offered the asking price.

- This outcome led to more confidence about trusting my GUT, the Realtor trusting his GUT, and both of us thinking outside of the box for future marketing ideas.

It is that easy. Take the first step of confidence, however small. Delight in finding a creative and unique approach, and think outside the box. With this initial success under your belt, take the next step of confidence and creativity. One day, you will look back and see how your life has moved from reactivity to proactivity.

Intuition is seeing with the soul.
—DEAN KOONTZ

Self-confidence is the first requisite
to great undertakings.
—SAMUEL JACKSON

Intuition is really a sudden immersion of the
soul into the universal current of life.
—PAULO COELHO, THE ALCHEMIST

Don't let the noise of other people's opinions
drown out your own inner voice.
—STEVE JOBS

Ask yourself these questions. Again, take notes, as it increases your retention of material by 87 percent.

Ask yourself...

What is a negative/reactive cycle that I would like to begin turning around in my life? Start small, with something safe with which to test the waters.

What are the conscious choices and intentions that you want to create outcomes for in your life?

_____

_____

_____

_____

Example: For me, with the real estate story, the negative cycle that I chose to turn around was not allowing others opinions to squelch my inner voice.

Identify the action(s) that you want to take.

_____

_____

_____

_____

Example: Write my GUT instinct on the asking price down. Ask for Realtor referrals.

Think outside the box. What creative approach can you implement to get the result you want?

_____

_____

_____

_____

Example: Realtor referrals are not working. Maybe I need to give a newly licensed Realtor who is hungry a chance at listing this property.

Example: The property is near the Sierra Nevada Mountains in California. Perhaps we need to market to San Francisco proper as well.

Congratulations! You have with clear, conscious choice and intention just created your first "Confidence and Creation" cycle.

It is that simple. Let's move on now to the letter T in ACT.

Change your thoughts, change your world.
—**Vincent Norman Peale**

With our thoughts we make the world.
—**Buddha**

Nothing is impossible. The word
itself says "I'm possible."
—**Audrey Hepburn**

Strength doesn't come from what you can do.
It comes from overcoming what you
thought you couldn't do.
—**Rikki Rogers**

Whether you think you can, or you
think you can't—you're right.
—**Henry Ford**

Hold every thought captive.
—**Saint Paul**

The greatest weapon against stress is the ability
to choose one thought over the other.
—**William James**

Think about what is true, noble, right,
pure, lovely, admirable, and excellent.
—**Philippians 4:8**

T = Turning GUT Instincts into Action

Turning your instincts into action is where Nike's motto "Just do it" comes into play. At this point you have identified your authentic GUT instinct(s). You have made conscious choices about your intentions, resulting in the outcomes that you want. Now you will turn these instincts into action simply by acting on them: "doing it." You are now hearing your inner voice—listening to, trusting, and acting on your GUT instinct(s). This is where the transformational power of your new outcomes shows up tangibly in your life!

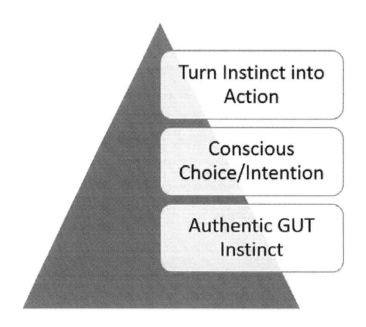

Here is another tool that has helped me, and can help you too. Whenever I see a stoplight, it reminds me of a practice that I weave into my life in order to be proactive with Instinctology®. **I stop, breathe, and then act.**

The red color at the top of the stoplight reminds me to stop.
The yellow color in the center of the stoplight reminds me to wait and breathe.
The green color at the bottom of the stoplight reminds me to go—to act.

Congratulations! You are on your way to mastering *Instinctology®: A Leadership Method to Turn GUT Instincts into Concrete Action.*

What you get by achieving your goals
is not as important as what you
become by achieving your goals.
—HENRY DAVID THOREAU

Anyone who has never made a mistake
has never tried anything new.
—ALBERT EINSTEIN

The person who says something is impossible
should not interrupt the person who is doing it.
—CHINESE PROVERB

The secret to getting started is getting started.
—MARK TWAIN

Just do it!
—NIKE'S MOTTO

Watch your thoughts; they become words.
Watch your words; they become actions.
Watch your actions; they become habit.
Watch your habits; they become character.
Watch your character; it becomes your destiny.
—UNKNOWN

CHAPTER 5

Your Actions Matter! Getting Results That Make a Difference

B acked by the Instinctology® stories and with the three proven action steps in the acronym ACT, you are on your way to making *Instinctology®: A Leadership Method to Turn GUT Instincts into Concrete Action* a game-changing lifestyle. As illustrated in the diagrams below, initially you will practice Instinctology® with deliberate intention, using ACT. Over time, practicing Instinctology® will become second nature to you. Automatically your proactive response for how you lead yourself and others will flow from your GUT instincts.

Deliberate and Intentional Instinctology®

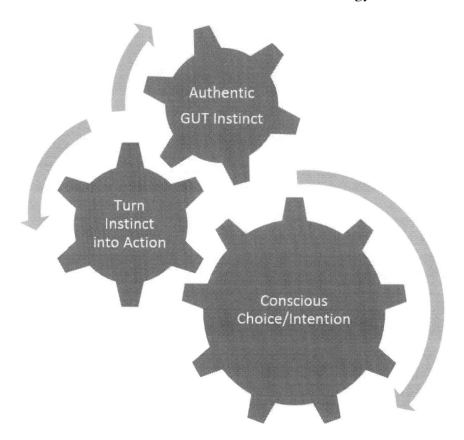

Second Nature Instinctology®
(Your Leadership Lifestyle)

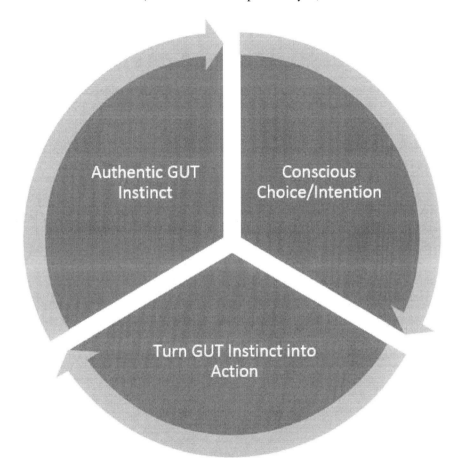

Mastering Instinctology® will make an extraordinary difference in your life. You will excel at leading yourself and others. You will outdo yourself while getting the results you need. Finally, you will make an impressive impact for the highest good of yourself and others. You can do this!

Closing Thoughts

What is your Instinctology® story? Your story could be the turning point and inspiration for someone to get started mastering Instinctology®. To share your story and to access Instinctology® services/resources, please go to the website at **www.instinctology.com.**

Remember, we are one together. Together we can make the world a better place as we learn to lead from our GUT instincts!

Lead from your GUT instincts,
Roben Graziadei, MA
Best-selling author, speaker, coach, and workshop leader
Instinctology®: A Leadership Method to Turn GUT Instincts into Concrete Action

And those who were seen dancing were thought
insane by those could not hear the music.
—Friedrich Nietzche

Have the courage to follow your heart
and intuition. They somehow already
know what you truly want to become.
Everything else is secondary.
—Steve Jobs

Every moment is a moment of decision,
and every moment turns us inexorably in
the direction of the rest of our lives.
—Mary Bilogh

Thinking is easy; acting is difficult; and
to put one's thoughts into action is the
most difficult thing in the world.
—Goethe

ABOUT THE AUTHOR

Roben Graziadei, MA
Chief Instinctology® Officer
CEO/founder, Net Result$, LLC

Roben Graziadei is the founder and president of Net Result$ and is a highly successful speaker and management consultant. Her book *Instinctology®: A Leadership Method to Turn GUT Instincts into Concrete Action* can change your life forever, bringing lasting change with sustained results.

Having consulted with the C-suite and boards of many Fortune 500 companies and higher education institutions, Roben then trained over 500,000 people from the mail room to the boardroom. Her client list includes Google, Bank of America, Nordstrom, PG&E, the Gap, the Sharper Image, Advanced Micro Devices, Chevron Corporation, Microsoft, Safeway, Seagate Technologies, Autodesk, Hewlett Packard, Bristol Myers Squibb, Tandem Computers, Remedy Corporation, Oracle, McKesson, Merrill Lynch, Lucky Stores, Kaiser Permanente, Peoplesoft, Household Credit Services, and California State Parole Officers, to name a few.

Roben has developed strong leaders and work units at all levels through consulting and training, including outdoor adventure courses in leadership excellence, values-based time management, sales training, and business development. Through these efforts, she has consistently enabled her clients to increase customer satisfaction and sales revenue results. Clients can expect to see quarterly sales increases of as much as 31 percent over the prior year following the principles she lives by and teaches. Many clients have enjoyed double-digit sales increases year over year.

Roben began her career as a senior consultant with FranklinCovey. She is thrilled to return to this top-rated leadership company and is currently a sales executive/client partner with FranklinCovey. Roben was also a principal of the Tom Peters Group Learning Systems. Earlier in her career, while in product development for Foodmaker, Inc., she was on the team that created and introduced the Pita-Pocket Supreme sandwich, an original healthy fast-food item, which created a new market niche for the fast-food industry.

Roben has a BS in business administration and an MA in psychology and graduated with distinction. Her passion for business is evidenced by the kudos she receives from her audiences and repeated requests to return for consulting engagements. Participants describe her as a dynamic and compelling facilitator who is knowledgeable on many levels, as well as being humorous and fun. An outdoor enthusiast, Roben winters in Arizona and summers in Colorado with her family.

Disclaimer

Instinctology® is not a substitute for seeking help needed by a health care professional. Neither Net Result$, LLC nor the author are responsible for the medical or mental health of any persons that access or participate in Instinctology® via our course(s), keynotes, books, social media or any other resource. These are the author's opinions and stories of her success. Results are not a guarantee.

Made in the USA
San Bernardino, CA
20 May 2017